BE PREPARED!

The Frankie MacDonald Guide to Life, the Weather, and Everything

Frankie MacDonald and Sarah Sawler

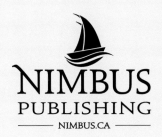

NIMBUS
PUBLISHING
— NIMBUS.CA —

For Mike, who's always there to support me, no matter what.
—Sarah

For my grandparents, my aunt and uncle, and my father.
—Frankie

Nimbus Publishing Limited
3660 Strawberry Hill Street, Halifax, NS, B3K 5A9
(902) 455-4286 nimbus.ca

Printed and bound in Canada
NB1355
Design: Grace Laemmler Design
Cover photo: Vaughan Merchant

Library and Archives Canada Cataloguing in Publication
MacDonald, Frankie, 1984-, author
Be prepared! : the Frankie MacDonald guide to life, the weather, and everything / Frankie MacDonald and Sarah Sawler.

Issued in print and electronic formats.
ISBN 978-1-77108-575-5 (softcover).—ISBN 978-1-77108-576-2 (HTML)

1. Weather—Miscellanea. I. Sawler, Sarah, author II. Title.

QC981.2.M33 2018   551.6   C2017-907991-3
                              C2017-907992-1

Nimbus Publishing acknowledges the financial support for its publishing activities from the Government of Canada, the Canada Council for the Arts, and from the Province of Nova Scotia. We are pleased to work in partnership with the Province of Nova Scotia to develop and promote our creative industries for the benefit of all Nova Scotians.

TABLE OF CONTENTS

Frankie recording one of his famous YouTube videos.

INTRODUCING... FRANKIE MACDONALD!

FRANKIE MACDONALD loves the weather. He loves everything about it, from snowstorms and tornadoes to heat waves and windstorms. He enjoys studying it, talking about it, and monitoring it, but most of all, he loves sharing his weather forecasts with the entire world through his YouTube channel, dogsandwolves.

Frankie started using YouTube in 2006, not long after the video-sharing platform was launched. Now, more than one hundred and seventy thousand people subscribe to his YouTube channel. And that number doesn't include the people who just occasionally watch his videos. His subscribers are people who like Frankie so much that they want to be notified every time he puts up a new video.

It took a long time for Frankie to get to where he is now, but now that he's here, life is pretty exciting. Not only do plenty of people watch his videos on YouTube, but he also has lots of followers on social media, and his weather forecasts are played on news stations all over North America.

I do my videos to warn people when there is a major storm headed their way, like a hurricane, a blizzard, a big rainstorm, and hailstorms.
— Frankie

Most people agree that Frankie's weather forecasts are pretty amazing. Not only are his forecasts helpful, because they're often accurate, but Frankie always seems really happy and excited to talk about the weather with everyone watching his videos.

When Frankie's YouTube channel started getting really popular, people began interviewing him for newspapers, TV, podcasts, and radio stations. His first big news interview was in February 2013, when Frankie was twenty-eight years old. The interview was with CBC reporter Gary Mansfield, who lives in Sydney, Cape Breton, just like Frankie. In the interview they talked a lot about Frankie's success, and also about his experiences with online bullying.

What is meteorology?
Britannica Kids explains meteorology like this: "The weather on Earth is always changing. Meteorology is a field of science that studies the changes in weather on a day-to-day basis in a specific place. Scientists who study meteorology are called meteorologists. Using various tools, meteorologists forecast whether it will rain or snow and whether it will be warm or cold."

Frankie has autism, and sometimes he behaves differently than some other people do. Autism is a neurodevelopmental disorder, which is a fancy name for disorders that keep someone's brain or nervous system from growing and developing in a typical way. Autism is also a "spectrum," which means this disorder causes different combinations of behaviours in different people. Sometimes, you might hear people say a person with autism is "on the autism spectrum," and that just means that the person has been diagnosed with autism. Frankie's autism makes it difficult for him to communicate (though not so

What are weather models and how do they work?

Weather models are actually computer programs. Weather stations all over the world and satellites up in space track things like snowfall, windchill, low pressure systems, and more. Then all this information is sent to these computer programs, which use this information to do a lot of complicated math.

These math equations are designed to predict how the weather will change in the future. Once all these calculations are done (some of the supercomputers that do this work can make 50 to 100 trillion calculations per second), the programs provide information (data) that can be used by people like Frankie, who know how to read them, to forecast the weather.

difficult now as it was in his younger years), and to form relationships with other people.

Although most people love Frankie, sometimes people make fun of him. In the interview with Gary Mansfield, his aunt, Darlene MacDonald, said something very important about the way those people talk to and about Frankie: "It's very, very hurtful," she told the reporter. "They wouldn't speak like that if it was their relative or their son. Basically, they don't know what autism is and they don't realize [those with autism] have feelings too." She also said that "when it comes to technology, Frankie is gifted."

She's right about that. Not only did Frankie figure out how to use—and master—YouTube when it was still brand new, he also taught himself to read weather models (see the box at the top of this page) and patterns (technical stuff you need to

Frankie looking at an online weather model.

> Winter is my favourite season because I get to do a lot of weather forecasting online to warn people about blizzards, ice storms, and extreme cold weather. I try to help people, to prevent car accidents and other dangers.
> — Frankie

understand in order to predict the weather). Now he's able to accurately predict the weather a lot of the time.

A lot of people don't realize this, but sometimes, if someone studies really hard like Frankie does, they can teach themselves how to understand things like meteorology (see sidebar on page 4). In addition to reading the weather models and patterns, Frankie also monitors the local weather using a portable weather station that's set up on his back deck, and he checks the weather all over the world using his smart phone, and sometimes his computer.

Frankie's even received a couple of awards for his hard work, including a 2014 Cape Breton Vital Excellence Award, which celebrated his work as a "weatherman and Cape Breton Ambassador." He's also received a Silver Creator Award from YouTube—which is really special because YouTube only gives those to YouTubers with more than one hundred thousand subscribers.

Although Frankie loves to talk about the weather, that's not the only reason he makes his videos. He makes them because he wants to help people get ready when bad weather is coming—he wants them to "Be Prepared!" In 2015, a Cape Breton Member of Parliament, Mark Eyking, recognized Frankie in the House of Commons. According to a CBC

Frankie's Storm Preparation Advice

"If there's a big storm coming, stay inside and make sure animals are inside. Buy things like bottled water and extra groceries and extra batteries and battery-operated lanterns and emergency kits before the big huge storm hits."

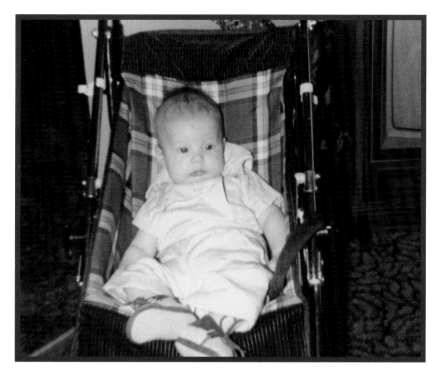

Baby Frankie in 1984, all ready to go exploring.

News article, Mr. Eyking said, "I rise today to recognize weatherman extraordinaire Mr. Frankie MacDonald of Whitney Pier, Nova Scotia. We as Cape Bretoners are very proud of Frankie the Weatherman and wish him all the best as he continues to keep us safe from Mother Nature."

Now, Frankie is so popular, he has a series of bobbleheads—including one that really talks—an action figure, and even T-shirts with a couple of his catchphrases printed on them ("Get Your Chinese Food!" and "Frankie Says Be Prepared"). But although his life is very exciting now, like most lives, it started out in a much quieter way.

Frankie was born in 1984 in Sydney, Cape Breton. His parents didn't live together when Frankie was born, and they didn't plan to live together after he was born either, so they had to decide if Frankie would live with his dad, or his mom, or both of them on different days. Frankie's parents made their decision, and when baby Frankie left the hospital, he went home with his dad.

This is the story of what happened next.

1 FINDING HIS VOICE

FRANKIE LOVES talking to people, but he had to work hard to get good at it. When he was three, he went to a daycare in Sydney called the Children's Training Centre. These days most kids go to school and learn together, no matter what their abilities are, but in 1987, when Frankie

Young Frankie, having fun posing for the camera.

was three, it didn't always happen that way. Some schools and daycares, like the Children's Training Centre, only took care of children with neurodevelopmental disorders like autism. Frankie went there for four years, and although he played with other kids, he couldn't really talk to them—he could only say a few words. He sometimes tried to talk to people by making noises.

Many people with autism have a hard time talking to other people, and some don't talk to others at all. This definitely doesn't mean they aren't smart—because autistic people are just as smart as people who aren't autistic. People with autism just think in a different way—often using pictures instead of words. For example, while many people think in words, like, "I really want a grilled cheese sandwich for lunch," some people with autism may think of a picture of a grilled cheese sandwich on a plate in their kitchen. This is called "visual thinking." It's a lot easier for some people to share their thoughts using pictures and sign language than words.

> **What do these words mean, again?**
> **Neurodevelopmental disorder** is a scientific name for a group of disorders that keep someone's brain or nervous system from growing and developing in a typical way. Some examples include autism, attention-deficit/hyperactivity disorder, and learning disabilities.
>
> Autism is sometimes called "**the autism spectrum**" because it causes different combinations of experiences and behaviour in different people. There are a few common behaviours associated with autism: challenges communicating and forming relationships, and repetitive behaviour.

Have you ever seen one of Frankie's interviews with Fred the Teddy Bear? Fred always has interesting adventures, but he had some humble beginnings. "I found Fred in my grandmother's house, down in the basement," says Frankie. "He first appeared in a video in 2011."

Frankie, celebrating his eleventh birthday at McDonalds.

When Frankie turned seven, he left his daycare and started going to Ashby Elementary School in Sydney. Kids with all different kinds of abilities went to the school, but Frankie joined a unique class that only taught kids who were similar to him. There, he learned math and reading, science and music, plus lots of other things. He even went swimming and bowling once a week. He was especially good at math and memorizing things. Frankie's class also had time to play—and he usually chose to play with blocks and build bridges.

Learning about autism

Have you ever seen another kid start banging their head, maybe on their desk or the wall, but there doesn't seem to be a reason for it? Or maybe you've noticed someone else flapping their hands beside their ears? Maybe you even do these things yourself! If so, you might have wondered why this happens. There's a good reason for it: for some people on the autism spectrum, this is a way of trying to cope with stressful situations.

Here's where it gets tricky. Often, situations that are stressful for people on the autism spectrum aren't the same kinds of situations that are stressful for people who don't have autism. That's because people with autism sometimes experience sights, sounds, textures, tastes, and smells differently. A light might seem a lot brighter, a blanket could feel a lot scratchier, or a cookie might taste a lot sweeter. If too many things are happening at once, a person with autism might start feeling really overwhelmed, to the point where their thoughts and emotions feel all mixed up. Some people actually feel pain when there's too much happening around them. This is called "sensory overload."

Before long, a teacher's aide named Mrs. Simms started helping out in the class every Friday. The first time Mrs. Simms walked into Frankie's classroom, she sat down right next to Frankie and he started banging his head on his desk. When Frankie was young, he did this whenever he felt scared, nervous, or sometimes just overwhelmed. But Mrs. Simms understood, so she went and talked with some other children and gave Frankie a bit of time to get used to having her around. After a few days, she started sitting with Frankie and some of his friends at lunchtime. He started to feel more comfortable around Mrs. Simms, and sometimes he felt safe enough to answer her questions by nodding his head.

Frankie had started working with a speech therapist when he was in daycare. A speech therapist is a person who helps people improve their speaking and communication skills, so this was a great solution for Frankie, because talking was still very difficult for him. Over time, the speech therapist helped him learn to say more words—but only when he felt safe and comfortable with the person he was talking to.

Soon, Frankie started to really enjoy spending time with Mrs. Simms. He liked her so much that sometimes he felt sad on days when she wasn't there. They went for walks together

Fast Frankie Fact
The wettest place on Earth is Mawsynram, Meghalaya, India, with an average of 11,873 millimetres of rain per year. That's almost 11.8 metres in total!

What's sensory overload?

Imagine you're playing outside, and you get a splinter in your foot. It hurts a lot, right? But then you fall off your bike and scrape your knee. That hurts more! But you probably wouldn't notice the splinter as much anymore, would you? Of course not, because you're more focused on your knee. That's why some people on the autism spectrum bang their heads—because the head pain distracts from the overwhelming thoughts and feelings or the pain caused by all the different things happening around them.

When Frankie was little, he felt overwhelmed a lot. And when he did, he sometimes coped with it by banging his head, punching his leg, biting his arm, or flapping his hands by his ears. Even though Frankie is a lot older now, he stills remembers those times. A lot of the time, he was very happy. But sometimes, he says, life was stressful for him.

"I had some hard times when I was little," he says. Now that he's bigger, he has an easier time with those overwhelming, stressful feelings. As he got older, he stopped hurting himself as often. And now that he's a grown-up, he can tell when he's feeling overwhelmed. "I rest," Frankie says. "Makes me feel better."

at lunchtime and recess, and sometimes Frankie would hold Mrs. Simms's hand. Other times, Frankie would talk a bit, or he'd sing songs as they walked around the playground. Mrs. Simms still remembers a song Frankie used to sing to her, about a bird that was sitting in a tree and then flew away. Once, Mrs. Simms showed Frankie how to play hopscotch.

Frankie was already interested in the weather during those early years. After he got upset one day, Mrs. Simms decided to try and help him calm down by reading a book with him. He chose a book about farm animals. They turned the pages, and Frankie stopped on page three. Carefully, he took Mrs. Simms's finger and placed it over the sky in the picture. Then he told her it was a sunny day.

> # I love the sunshine the most.
> # — Frankie

Before long, Frankie had to go to a new school—he was nine, and so he was ready to start going to Sydney River Elementary School. He had a new teacher, Mrs. Sampson, twelve new kids in his class,

Why do we have seasons?

Billions of years ago, the Earth was hit by something really big. Scientists don't know for sure what it was, but many of them think Earth was hit by another planet. The crash tipped the Earth over a bit, which means the Earth's axis, a straight line that connects the North Pole to the South Pole, doesn't point straight up and down anymore—it points a little to the side, like this. That's the Earth's tilt.

Because the Earth rotates around the sun (it makes a trip around the sun every 365 days), different parts of the Earth are tilted towards the sun at different times of year. That's why we have seasons. When your part of the Earth is tilted as close as it can get to the sun, it's summer. And when your part of the Earth is tilted as far away from the sun as it can get, it's winter! That's why it can be winter in Australia (south of the equator) and summer in Canada (north of the equator) at the same time!

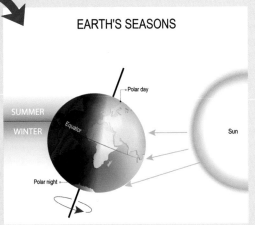

EARTH'S SEASONS

With his helmet, knee pads, and elbow pads, Frankie's ready to learn to rollerblade!

and a new school to get used to. Frankie feels happiest when he's with people he knows, in a place he's used to, so the new experience was a little scary for him at first. But then something exciting happened—Mrs. Simms started working at his new school, and helping Frankie became part of her job! Frankie says he felt great when Mrs. Simms showed up.

That year, Frankie still had trouble paying attention for long stretches of time, and sometimes he had a really hard time staying in his seat. But having a teacher's aide who he knew and trusted really helped, because Mrs. Simms understood that Frankie was really smart, and the fact that he was wiggly and sometimes had trouble talking didn't change that.

Frankie was still working hard on his math, reading, and spelling. Usually, Mrs. Simms would correct his work and return it to him, then give him a day to figure out what he'd gotten wrong. Then he'd try again. The second time, he always had the right answers—but sometimes he put them in the wrong spots. That's because Frankie has a photographic memory, which means that when he sees something, he can picture it in his head again later, whenever he needs to

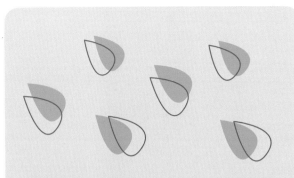

Why does it rain?

Have you ever left a glass of water out on a hot day, only to discover that some of it is gone a few hours later? When water gets warm, it evaporates, which means it turns into vapour and rises into the air.

While the vapour rises, it condenses, meaning that it cools down and turns back into a liquid. These tiny water droplets form clouds. When the clouds get too full, those water droplets start connecting with each other, causing them to turn into bigger water droplets. When *those* droplets get big and heavy enough, they fall from the clouds as rain.

remember a small detail. This is one of the reasons Frankie is so good at remembering the weather facts and information he's learned over the years!

Math was one of Frankie's favourite subjects, and he was always one of the first kids to turn in his assignments. He wasn't rushing and being careless, though, because he almost always got the answers right. The other kids were usually really impressed. Mrs. Simms sat with Frankie during math tests, just in case he got distracted and needed her to get him back on track. But she never had to remind him to pay attention when he was doing math. He loved math so much he was easily able to focus all on his own.

School really started to go well for Frankie the year he turned ten, and it just got better from there. He started speech therapy with a new teacher, and worked really hard at it. He started speaking more and more, and soon, everyone in Frankie's life, from his dad to Mrs. Simms, noticed a big difference. His speech therapist really liked working with him, and said he "got along just great."

Frankie also started to have an easier time staying in his seat and working by himself—without Mrs. Simms's help. At recess and lunch, he began making friends. He especially loved it when his friends would push him on the swing outside. Remember how he banged his head on his desk when he first met Mrs. Simms? He'd mostly stopped doing that by now, too. All of this, plus the fact that he'd learned to speak in sentences, made it easier for Frankie to get to know the other kids.

2 MAP QUEST

IF YOU WANT to learn about the weather, it helps a lot if you're good at geography, which is a science that focuses on the Earth's physical features—from mountains and lakes to countries and continents—as well as its climate, and population. Frankie started learning about geography when he was really little. When he was just four years old, he loved street signs simply because they had the names of the streets written on them. It helped that he liked signs a lot in general. This might be because he's a visual thinker (he thinks in pictures instead of sentences), so signs that provide information using symbols instead of words would perfectly fit his way of thinking!

"Frankie used to carry around a cardboard stop sign," says Frankie's grandmother, Rose MacDonald. "I remember when it broke in half—we had to tape it back together again."

About four years later, Frankie began reading and collecting maps and atlases. He started by learning about his own city, Sydney, Cape Breton, and as soon as he memorized all of its streets and their locations, he started learning about a new area.

Have you ever looked closely at a street map? The streets are often arranged in squares (but not always). The pattern

Frankie shows off his map collection.

these streets make when you look at them from above is called a "grid." Frankie studied these grids and memorized where all the streets were in a lot of different places, even in places as far away as Europe. He studied these maps so carefully that when he went on vacation, he knew his way around—even if he'd never been to the place before! His grandmother says she loved going on trips with Frankie because as long as he was around, they never got lost.

Frankie's map collection is enormous. His dad bought him maps. His grandparents bought him maps. Even Mrs. Simms, his teacher's aide in elementary school, bought him maps for Christmas after he started talking about geography with her at recess. Sometimes he quizzed Mrs. Simms, asking her questions like, "Mrs. Simms, if you were stranded on Benson Drive, where would you have to go?" Then Mrs. Simms would

Which places in the world have the hottest weather?

Death Valley, California, holds the world record for the highest air temperature ever recorded, at 56.7 degrees Celsius, on July 10, 1913. In Furnace Creek, which is in Death Valley, it's so hot that the average temperature is about 46 degrees Celsius. That's the same temperature you'd use to cook a rare steak! Furnace Creek seems like a pretty appropriate name now, doesn't it?

Outside of California, some of the world's hottest temperatures can be found in:

- **Dasht-e Lut, Iran:** the hottest ground temperature ever recorded here was 70.7 degrees Celsius in 2005.
- **El Azizia, Libya:** this town once reached 57.7 degrees Celsius.
- **Dallol, Ethiopia:** this town has the highest average temperatures of any inhabited place on Earth. From 1960 to 1966, daily temperatures reached up to 34 degrees Celsius.

Landscape of sand dunes in Death Valley, California.

Which places in the world have the coldest weather?

That depends! Oymyakon, a small village in Russia's Siberian tundra, is the coldest inhabited place on earth. The village earned its status in 1933, when temperatures dropped to -67.8 degrees Celsius. In 2017, the village put up a giant digital thermometer that shows the temperature all the time. Unfortunately, not long after they put it up, the weather got so cold that the thermometer broke!

The coldest temperature ever recorded was in Vostok Station, Antarctica, in 1983. On that date, temperatures dropped to -89.2 degrees Celsius. Brrrr!

Oymyakon, Siberia

have to use her imagination and her knowledge of Sydney to figure out where she would go.

Fast Frankie Fact

Did you know that the Eiffel Tower in Paris is 15 centimetres taller in the summer than it is in the winter? That's because it's made of iron. Cold weather makes iron contract (shrink), and warm weather makes iron expand (get bigger).

Frankie played map games with his dad, too. Sometimes, they'd use the maps to go "monster hunting" in the car. Frankie would be in the house, playing with blocks or looking at a book, and his dad would run into the room with news: "Frankie! I just heard a report that there's a monster in Point Aconi!" And Frankie would be up and out the door, road map in hand. Then they'd go for a drive together, and Frankie would use his map to give his dad directions to wherever Frankie thought the imaginary monster was. (NOTE: There wasn't really a monster, they were just pretending. Monsters aren't real. Unless little brothers who eat your candy when you aren't looking count. Do they count?)

Frankie's favourite weather spots

"I think the United States of America has the most interesting weather, because there are a lot of tornadoes, blizzards, severe thunderstorms, hurricanes, and tropical cyclones. There are also lots of snowstorms in the Central Great Plains (that's Ohio, Indiana, Illinois, Michigan, Wisconsin, Minnesota, Iowa, and Missouri), and big rainstorms in California."

Summer gale in South Haven, Michigan.

Thunderstorm in Cleveland, Ohio.

When Frankie got older, he started ordering his own street maps at the bookstore. Today, his collection includes maps of all the cities in Canada, lots of major US cities, and some European countries. Of course, now Frankie also spends a lot of time on Google Maps. He looks at places all over the world, zooming in on highways, checking out the traffic, seeing if there's snow on the side of the road. He just wants to know what it all looks like. And he's learned a lot. Frankie's dad, Frank, says, "the things Frankie knows about the world is beyond what most people can comprehend. He can tell you almost anything about the world."

Frankie loves sports. In this picture, he's wearing a Toronto Blue Jays baseball cap.

3 WEATHER WATCHER

FRANKIE STARTED watching the weather channel when he was just a toddler. His dad, Frank, has always been interested in the weather too, so sometimes Frank would turn on the TV and leave the weather channel on, just to have some background noise in the house. Of course, Frankie's dad would pay attention to it here and there—like Frankie, Frank understands weather patterns and knows how to read the satellite images. But Frankie would sit on the floor and watch the weather for long periods of time.

My favourite weather fact is that when warm, moist air meets cold Arctic air in the winter months, it can cause a big nor'easter, which is a type of cyclone that usually comes with heavy rain or snow. In the summer, severe thunderstorms or even tornadoes can happen when warm, moist air meets cold Arctic air.
— Frankie

At first, it was probably the maps and satellite colours that caught little Frankie's attention, but his dad soon realized that Frankie was actually learning from what he was watching. "I would never have thought anything of it," says Frank. "But he was absorbing a lot."

As he got older, Frankie started getting really interested in watching weather news, especially when it had to do with storms. And he didn't just watch local forecasts—he also watched national and international forecasts.

When Frankie eventually got a computer (most people didn't have computers in their homes until the late 1980s or so), he did a lot of research on the internet. In 2007, Frankie started studying weather models. He says he particularly liked learning about tornadoes, hail, damaging winds, thunderstorms, and things like that. "I was curious to find out what was happening in the world," Frankie says.

Frankie always wanted to be a meteorologist when he grew up, so he taught himself as much as he could. "Those other professionals that are around, they have education," he says. "I studied the weather models like rainfall, snowfall, wind speed.... That means the sun, cloud, rain, things like that. Hurricanes, tornadoes." He even included the weather in his artwork. Mrs. Simms remembers a placemat that Frankie made at school. On the placemat, he drew a plane flying through a thunder and lightning storm. He told her the plane was going to the BWK hospital—but he meant the IWK Health Centre in Halifax.

What do you want to be when you grow up?

Whether you want to be a meteorologist, an artist, or a veterinarian, you're never too young to start learning. Frankie says that if you know what you want to be when you grow up, "You have to keep learning, even when it gets hard."

How hot is lightning?

When lightning hits the air, the air can reach 29,727 degrees Celsius. That's more than five times hotter than the surface of the sun, which is 5,500 degrees Celsius! And it's almost twenty-four times hotter than the hottest lava, which can reach up to 1,160 degrees Celsius.

Even though Frankie knows a lot about predicting the weather, sometimes storms are unpredictable. Hurricane Joaquin is a perfect example. This hurricane formed in 2015, and it was very strong. It was a category 4 hurricane, which means the wind could be moving as fast as 249 kilometres

Frankie tries on his uncle's high school graduation cap and gown.

per hour. That's fast enough to blow down a small house! Frankie says Joaquin was very difficult to forecast—it was supposed hit the Eastern seaboard of the United States, and it ended up turning towards Bermuda instead, so Frankie had to cancel his forecast. Unfortunately, because of climate change, the weather is becoming more and more unpredictable, which means that meteorologists are having a more difficult time forecasting the weather.

Watching the weather on TV was one thing, but when storms were close to home, they sometimes scared Frankie when he was young. Mrs. Simms remembers a day, at Ashby Elementary School, that was particularly scary for Frankie. His class went swimming every Friday, and one day before swimming it got really windy outside. Frankie's class was about to get on the bus to go to the pool, but the high winds scared him a lot.

What is climate change?

That's a big question, and the answer is so complicated that lots of adults still don't understand. It all starts with the sun, which keeps planet Earth warm enough for us to live on it. The Earth stays warm partly because of greenhouse gases (like carbon dioxide, methane, and nitrous oxide), which are naturally in the Earth's atmosphere. They help trap the heat in like a warm blanket on a cold night.

The trouble is, the amount of greenhouse gases in our atmosphere is now very high, because lots of things humans do—like driving cars, using electricity, running factories, even raising cows—release extra greenhouse gases into the atmosphere. Now that nice cozy blanket is getting a little too warm. As a result, the Earth's temperatures are rising every year. That change in our atmosphere causes all kinds of crazy weather, like heat waves, wildfires, and even rising sea levels. For humans and many other species on the planet, climate change is definitely not a good thing. It can affect our health, our ability to grow and find food, and, in the case of wildfires and floods, even the places where we live.

Although the climate is already changing, there are still things you can do to help slow it down:

◗ **Turn off the lights when you aren't using them.**

◗ **Unplug your electronics when you're done with them.**

◗ **Drink tap water instead of bottled water.**

◗ **Turn off the tap when you brush your teeth.**

◗ **Make sure the tap is turned off when you leave the bathroom.**

◗ **Choose toys with less packaging.**

Can you think of other ways to fight climate change?

What's the difference between a tornado and a hurricane?

Tornadoes and hurricanes are both major storms that involve a lot of wind, but there are some big differences. Tornadoes are land-based. They take the shape of a funnel, and they form out of severe thunderstorms! They happen most often in the spring. One of the most interesting things about tornadoes is that you usually can't see them because they're made out of wind, which is invisible. They are a lot smaller than hurricanes and don't last as long: tornadoes can last as little as a few seconds and as long as a few hours.

Hurricanes, on the other hand, form over warm water and tend to hit coastal areas (places near the ocean) the hardest. They can also cause massive waves (called "storm surges") and a lot of flooding. They are much larger than tornadoes with higher wind speeds. In fact, tornadoes can sometimes form *inside* a hurricane!

When they're very strong, both tornadoes and hurricanes can cause a lot of damage to trees, houses, and people, so it's important to be prepared!

Frankie had seen a tornado on TV, so he was afraid the strong winds were actually part of that same tornado. He was still very young, so even though he spent a lot of time watching the weather on TV, he didn't quite understand that different places have different weather. The wind was blowing things around the schoolyard, and when a garbage can blew over, Frankie got really upset. He kept repeating "Tornado is coming!" and he was so scared that his teacher had to help him calm down by holding him. Frankie ended up skipping swimming that day and stayed with his teacher at school instead. When he got to class, he calmed down a lot, but his teacher could tell he was still afraid because he kept looking out the window and saying, "tornado."

Even though weather could be scary, Frankie also found it exciting, especially when he got older. He really liked to sit on the porch with his dad during thunder and lightning storms. From there, they had a good view of the Sydney Harbour. Sometimes

Frankie's Thunderstorm Advice

"Stay safe during thunderstorms by staying inside. If you have to go out, expect to get wet unless you wear your raincoat—you'll have to leave your umbrella at home. And never, ever go swimming outside during a thunderstorm! Metal (like in umbrellas) and water both conduct electricity, and make it possible to be struck by lightning."

Why don't we hear thunder and see lightning at the same time?

As you probably knew (or maybe guessed), thunder is the sound that lightning makes. But even though the thunder and lightning happen at the same time, it takes us longer to hear the thunder. That's because light travels faster than sound, which means that the sight of the lightning reaches our eyes before the sound of the thunder reaches our ears.

Fast Frankie Fact

Sometimes, animals like frogs and fish fall from the sky. Scientists think this happens when the animals are caught up in tornadoes and waterspouts (which are like tornadoes, but they form over water instead of land). After sucking the animals up, the tornado or waterspout takes them somewhere else. Then, when the wind dies down, the animals fall. This is what people think happened in 2010, when hundreds of little white fish fell from the sky in Lajamanu, Australia, and a large number of tiny frogs dropped on Rákóczifalva, Hungary, during a thunderstorm.

storms would cause waves in the harbour, and they really liked to watch those. During one really bad storm, Frankie's dad suggested they get in the car and go for a drive. "If the lightning didn't hit the car, it hit very close to us," Frankie's dad says. "It banged so hard. We just looked at each other and I just turned right around and drove back home again." Frankie's dad says it "took a lot to spook us because we love the weather, we love the storms." But he remembers another time the two of them got scared, during a downdraft, which is a big, sudden gust of wind that happens during thunderstorms. It happened when the pair was outside on the porch one night, and the wind blew so hard that the rain started blowing sideways instead of falling down. "It was going sideways in front of us and everything started to shake—because it takes a lot of force to send rain sideways," says Frankie's dad. The two of them jumped up and ran into the house.

4 BIKES AND BULLIES

SOMETIMES, FRANKIE'S stressful situations involved other kids. And although most kids were kind to Frankie, once in a while he'd run into a bully. That's what happened the day the school called Frankie's dad to tell him that Frankie had banged his head so hard he'd smashed it right through a window at school. Luckily, Frankie was okay in the end, but when the school tried to figure out why Frankie had done it, it turned out that another boy had teased Frankie until he felt so overwhelmed and frustrated that he started banging his head. It was a very long time ago, so no one remembers exactly what the other boy did to make Frankie so upset, but as Frankie's dad says, "Kids just picked on him sometimes."

When Frankie was twelve, his dad bought him his first bike. Some people didn't think that Frankie's dad should let him ride a bike because Frankie is autistic, and, for that same reason, they thought Frankie wouldn't able to do it. But Frankie's dad always let him try anything that the other kids got to do. Together, Frankie and his dad tried a lot of different things.

"I tried to teach him to play baseball but he'd just stand there with the bat, and wouldn't swing it," says Frank. "I took him tobogganing, and he loved the thrill of going down the hill, but it was work getting it back up. Same with the kite. He'd play with it for a couple of minutes and then he'd flap his hands by his ears and that was it. But the bike? That was a mode of transportation for him. He could get around all over the place."

When Frankie's dad bought him the bike, he made sure it had training wheels, but Frankie rode it so much the wheels started to bend, and soon they weren't even touching the ground anymore. Frankie was balancing and riding the bike all on his own!

Even though Frank let Frankie try lots of things, he still worried about his son riding his bike around by himself. This was partly because he was afraid that Frankie would get distracted and have an accident, and partly because he was nervous that a car might drive into him. So Frankie's dad was very careful to remind Frankie of two things:

1. To be careful not to run into people who are out walking.

2. To look out for cars, because the people driving them wouldn't always look out for him.

Frankie poses in his living room with the brand new bike he got for grading!

After Frankie had been riding his bike for a while without any accidents, his dad didn't worry as much. Frankie started riding around Whitney Pier and, as he got older, he went all over Sydney, often as far as five or seven kilometres away. He liked to explore the city, and he spent a lot of time riding around on the waterfront. One time, he rode his bike all the way to Sydney River—about nine kilometres away from home. The bike also gave Frankie the opportunity to talk to people he'd never met before.

Frankie enjoyed riding his bike for years and years, until he was about twenty-four years old, and he loved it every minute of it—until some kids stole his bike. Frankie's dad says they rode it over a bunch of rocks and smashed it up so badly that it wouldn't work anymore. Sadly, the whole experience scared Frankie so much that he wouldn't even let his dad buy him a new bike. He hasn't ridden a bike again since.

These days, it takes a lot to faze Frankie. Being internet-famous seems like a lot of fun, and for Frankie, it is, but it can also be tough—and sometimes scary. There are mean people on the internet, just like in real life. But on the internet, people are braver—maybe because no one can see them—and so sometimes they say hurtful things they would never say in real life. In fact, dogsandwolves wasn't Frankie's first YouTube channel—flank99 was. But he had to shut down flank99 back in 2010, because he says there were "too many negative people."

Of course, Frankie has thousands of fans, but some

Fast Frankie Fact

A tsunami is a long, massive wave that forms when an earthquake, volcanic eruption, or landslide happens underwater. The world's biggest recorded tsunami happened in Lituya Bay, Alaska, on July 9, 1958. That day, the wave was 524 metres high.

Got a bully? Get help.

Whether you're being bullied online or in school, start by talking to the bully and asking them to stop. Maybe they don't realize they're being mean! And if you need to get away quickly, you can turn off your computer or run away. "When a guy said, 'FRANKIE!' and stomped his feet in the schoolyard, I just ran," says Frankie.

But if that doesn't work, Frankie has some excellent advice for anyone being bullied: "They have to go to the teacher right away. They have to go to the principal's office. Or they have to talk to their parent, and their parent can talk to the bully's parent," he says. "They're picking on you because they're upset."

people also think it's cool to make fun of him. The more popular Frankie got and the more people viewed his videos, the nastier the comments and messages Frankie received. Sometimes other famous people even made fun of him. When this sort of thing happened, Frankie felt really sad, especially in the early days. In his interview with CBC in 2013, Frankie said that "people shouldn't be writing rude comments because they're not nice. They're rude, and they're disrespectful."

Frankie has been creating his YouTube videos for a long time now, though, and he's gotten a lot better at handling the mean people. He started dogsandwolves about a year after shutting down flank99, and he says he learned a lot from his first YouTube experience. "I ignore negative people and trolls. I ignore negative comments, I ignore rude comments," he says. "And I don't look at the mean emails, period. That's considered spam."

Stick up for your friends

When your friends are being bullied, it's important to help them. There are a couple of ways to do that: you can stand up to the bully and tell them to leave your friend alone, talk to a teacher or another adult you trust about what's happening to your friend, or you can just listen to your friend when they're upset.

Frankie has dealt with plenty of mean people over the years, and because he's a YouTuber, a lot of that bullying has happened online. That's called cyberbullying. Luckily, Frankie also has a lot of people looking out for him. A few years ago, a group called the Frankie Defence Team started up on Twitter, and now there are Frankie Defence Teams based in countries all over the world, including:

- NEW ZEALAND
- THE NETHERLANDS
- KAZAKHSTAN
- RUSSIA
- FRANCE
- UNITED STATES
- JAPAN

Why do some clouds look closer than others?

That's because they are! There are 10 basic types of clouds, and they all float at different levels in the sky. Cumulus, stratus, and stratocumulus clouds are in the first layer—they're the ones that hang closest to the ground. Altocumulus, nimbostratus, and altostratus clouds float above those ones. Cirrus, cirrocumulus, and cirrostratus clouds are another level up.

Cumulonimbus clouds are really special. They can be found at any level—close to the ground or fifty thousand feet in the air. That's much higher than any of the other clouds!

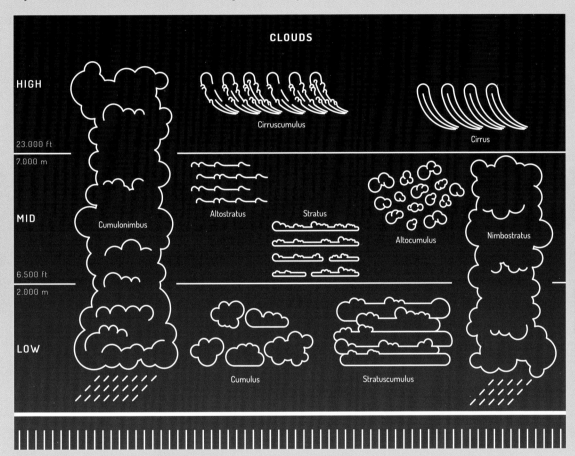

If clouds are full of rain, why do they float?

We know that clouds are full of water, and a bag of water is heavy, so it makes sense to wonder why that much water doesn't just fall out of the sky. But remember, clouds aren't one big blob of water, they're actually made up of tiny water droplets. And those water droplets are so tiny that gravity doesn't have much of an effect on them. So those water droplets float—until they get bigger and heavier, and turn into rain. Clouds can also move from place to place—that happens when the wind starts blowing all those water droplets around in the sky.

5 GAME ON

WHEN IT COMES TO TECHNOLOGY, Frankie's a natural. He's always been that way—if he picks up a piece of new technology, he's able to figure it out a lot quicker than most people could. His elementary school teacher's aide, Mrs. Simms, remembers the first time she saw him use a computer, and she says she was "really amazed" by how much he knew how to do.

Remember: today, most kids start using technology when they're toddlers. But that's not the way it was when Frankie was little. Computers were still new to a lot of people, and that meant people had to learn to use them. Those who have used computers for as long as they can remember—like you, probably—often have a pretty easy time figuring out new technology. If you're having trouble imagining what that would be like, just pretend you've never used a keyboard or a mouse before.

Fifteen-year-old Frankie, ready to get to work on his grandmother's computer.

Or imagine having to type out instructions to your computer, just to get it to start a new game. That's what it was like for most kids growing up in the 1980s.

But Frankie has always been good with computers, and he absolutely loves spending time on them. While Mrs. Simms watched him work, Frankie used the computer to spell out his first and last name, do addition and subtraction, and play a picture-matching game. "Frankie was in a whole other world, it seemed, on this computer," says Mrs. Simms.

Another time, Frankie's class learned how to make peanut butter: cracking the shells, putting them in the dish, and of course, eating lots. Frankie's job was operating the blender, and it didn't take him long at all to figure out how. The teacher would say "chop," and Frankie would chop. When she said "whip," he'd whip! Later, they all dipped apples and celery in the peanut butter they'd made—until Frankie got out the crackers. Of course, then everyone else wanted crackers too.

At home, Frankie liked to play video games. His dad enjoyed them too, so they got most of the popular consoles, all the way back to Atari, one of the first home video-game systems ever made. Together, Frankie and his dad played a lot of different games. They liked racing games a lot, especially Super Mario Kart. Of course, Frankie always wanted to be Mario. His dad often played with Donkey Kong. Frankie also liked role-playing games, like Final Fantasy, Zelda, and Tomb Raider. And he always completed them, from start to finish.

Best games ever

When Frankie was little, he played a lot of different video games, but he really loved playing the NHL games with his dad. "This was around when Frankie started to like the Senators, and develop his own opinions on sports," says his dad. "Once he understood the game, once he knew how to manipulate the controller and win, he was good. He had to have the new NHL games every year." But that wasn't all. Frankie also liked to play other games, like:

- TURTLES IN TIME
- SUPER MARIO BROS.
- ZELDA
- STAR FOX
- PILOTWINGS
- F-ZERO
- CASTLEVANIA

Frankie doesn't spend much time playing video games anymore, but when he does, he usually plays older games on his computer. He also likes to play games on his smart phone sometimes. Right now, his favourites are Bejeweled, Diamond Dash, and Tetris Blitz.

Frankie's dad wasn't quite as good at video games, but Frankie was always happy to help out. His dad remembers a time when Frankie, who was eleven or twelve at the time, was watching him play Tomb Raider. Frankie noticed things weren't going so well for his dad, so he made a suggestion: "Daddy needs cheat codes," he said.

"He didn't use them; he earned all his weapons," says Frank. "But he showed them to me, because it made the game a lot easier for me."

In 1992, when Frankie was eight, there was someone new to play video games with. Frankie's dad got married and bought a house a couple doors down from Frankie's grandparents' house. Frankie's new stepmom, Colleen, and her son, Steve, moved in with them. This was a really happy time for Frankie—he liked Colleen a lot, and he spent a lot of time with his new stepbrother, Steve. Steve is three years older than Frankie, but the two of them spent a lot of time playing video games together.

About nine years later, Frankie's dad and stepmom got a divorce, so Frankie and his dad moved into a new house nearby. That made it easy for Frankie to visit Colleen and Steve, so he was able to stay in close touch with them.

Frankie and his dad lived in that house for three years—until Frankie moved in with his grandmother. Just a couple of years later, Frankie discovered a whole new world of people to meet and things to learn. That's when his grandmother got a computer *and* an internet connection.

Just a couple days after Christmas 2007, that internet connection gave Frankie a way to start sharing his love of the weather with the world: he started taking photos of his local weather and sending them to The Weather Network.

Name game

Here's a fun fact: Did you know that Frankie and Stevie (which is what Frankie liked to call his stepbrother) actually share the same name? Frankie's real name is Stephen Francis, but people call him Frankie for short. And Stevie is a nickname too: his real name is also Stephen Francis!

Why do hurricanes and tropical storms have human names?

Meteorologists realized in the 1950s that naming hurricanes and tropical storms made them easier to talk about and easier for the average person to remember (especially when there's more than one storm happening in the same area of the world). Unofficially, people have been giving names to hurricanes for a long time, but we didn't come up with an official, long-term plan for naming Atlantic storms until 1953. That's when the National Hurricane Centre introduced a list of 26 women's names, one for each letter of the alphabet. The first storm of 1953 was Alice, the next storm was Barbara, the third storm was Carol, and so on.

Men's names were added to the lists in 1979. And other things have changed over the years, too. Now these lists of names are chosen by the World Meteorological Organization, and the lists no longer include names starting with the letters Q, U, X, Y, and Z, because there aren't enough names starting with those letters to go around.

Today, we use 6 different lists of 21 names, and they alternate between men's names and women's names. A different list is used each year, until we've gone through all 6 lists—then we start over again. Sometimes, though, the lists change. When a storm hurts a lot of people or damages a lot of property, the name of that storm is "retired" and replaced with a new name. One example of a retired name is Hurricane Katrina: the terrible 2005 hurricane that hit New Orleans in the US.

6 ACT FAST!

MOST PEOPLE KNOW who Frankie is because of his weather videos—because that's what people tend to ask him about in interviews. But he also loves to do comedy and dancing videos! In fact, one of his comedy videos, *Guy Tries to Eat 50 Hot Dogs at Once*, has been watched more than 1 million times. He has a lot of other comedy and dancing videos online too, including:

- ◗ *A Guy Dancing and Then Being Chased by Gorilla*
- ◗ *A Guy Dancing Then Raining Tacos*
- ◗ *The Guy Laughing Real Hard*
- ◗ *The Vampire Trying to Drink Tea*

He also does funny pretend weather reports, like *Severe Onion Rings Warning for Southern Australia* and *Cloudy with a Chance of Lobsters*.

Frankie has loved acting since high school, when he joined the Sydney Academy drama group. The group was run by Maynard Morrison, a teacher at the school who is also an

Frankie liked to watch his dad, Frank, play the drums. In this photo Frankie gets in on the act!

actor and comedian. Frankie learned a lot from him, especially when he acted in one of the plays Mr. Morrison wrote. Frankie played an alien, which was pretty exciting since he's really interested in the idea of aliens. He loved drama club, and if you watch his comedy and dancing videos now, it's clear that he still loves acting.

And it seems that performing runs in the family, because although Frankie's dad isn't an actor, he does love to write and perform music. Like Frankie, he practices a lot—and tries to write one new song every month. At least one of those songs was about Frankie. It's called "SuperFabPhenomenal" and it goes like this:

Fast Frankie Facts

🌭 His most-watched YouTube video is *Guy Tries to Eat 50 Hot Dogs at Once.*

🌭 The situations he chooses to act out in his comedy videos are all inspired by things he likes: hot dogs, aliens, and dancing included!

🌭 Frankie has never actually eaten 50 hot dogs at once.

SuperFabPhenomenal

When there's a change in the weather—no one tells it better
Delivered with true passion—like thunder comes a crashin'

When there's a chance of danger—the world is his neighbour
Nothin' to sell ya—he only wants to tell ya

He opens up his heart for you
Living his dream as he was born to do

SuperFabPhenomenal

Well, the temperature's risin'—dark cloud on the horizon
You better take shelter—a storm's in the smelter

When the rivers are raging—oh it never stops raining
He says, "Hey there, fella—don't forget your umbrella"

He opens up his heart for you
Living his dream as he was born to do

SuperFabPhenomenal

Stay inside, order your pizza pie
Take shelter, dude, order your Chinese food
When the storm clouds appear, you better take care

SuperFabPhenomenal

When there's a change in the weather—no one tells it better
Delivered with true passion—like thunder comes a crashin'

He opens up his heart for you
Living his dream as he was born to do

SuperFabPhenomenal

When it's cold, sometimes rain turns into snow. Other times, it turns into freezing rain or sleet. Why?

It all depends on how the temperature of the air changes as the rain (or snow) falls through the sky! All three kinds of precipitation start as snow, which forms when the air in the sky is cold enough to freeze water. If the air stays cold as the snow falls to the ground, we get snow.

If the air warms up as the snow falls, that snow turns to rain. If the air cools to freezing again for the last part of the journey, we get sleet, those little ice pellets that bounce when they hit the ground. But if the air only cools down to freezing again close to the ground, we get freezing rain. It's freezing rain that makes roads icy and gives tree branches that beautiful icy sparkle.

Hail is the scariest weather for me because it can break windows. Tornadoes are also very scary for me, same with blizzards and earthquakes.
—Frankie

Fast Frankie Fact

The biggest hailstone ever discovered in the US was found in Vivian, South Dakota, in July 2010. It was more than 45 centimetres around and weighed almost 1 kilogram!

7 ALL TOGETHER NOW

EVERYONE IS DIFFERENT. Some people like to spend a lot of time by themselves or with just a couple of their best friends. Others like to be around lots of people all the time. Although Frankie likes to spend time on his own, looking at weather models or studying maps or working on a new drawing, he also likes to spend a lot of time around other people.

That's part of the reason he spends so much time exploring. And it's also why Frankie enjoys going to movies and hockey games as much as he does—he likes sitting in the audience and enjoying the experience with other people.

When Frankie was fourteen or fifteen, his dad took him to see the Cape Breton Screaming Eagles. Frankie was already a hockey fan at the time—his dad liked the Montreal Canadiens, and Frankie did too. But around the

On the run

Have you ever wondered why Frankie decided to call his YouTube channel "dogsandwolves"? According to Frankie, the idea for the name came from an adventure he had while out for a walk one day. It was October 2008, and he was out walking on Victoria Road, near the boardwalk in Whitney Pier, when a couple of loose dogs started chasing him. Luckily for Frankie, those dogs got tired pretty quickly and Frankie was able to run away.

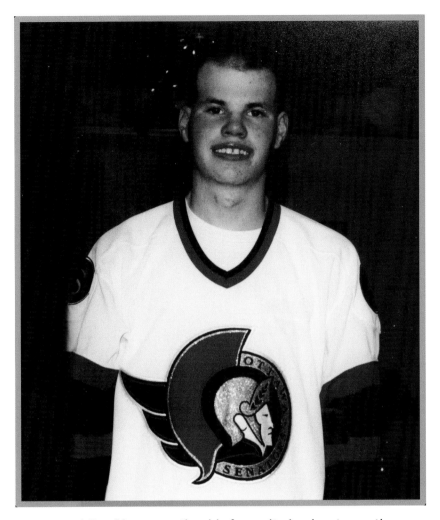

A teenaged Frankie supporting his favourite hockey team: the
Ottawa Senators!

same time Frankie and his dad started going to live games
together, Frankie decided he liked the Ottawa Senators better.
That's still his favourite team today.

Frankie didn't just go to hockey games for the game itself.
He also went for the hot dogs and the french fries. During
each intermission, his dad would get them snacks—and that
was a fun part of the routine.

Frankie still goes to
all the Screaming Eagles
games today, and he
watches basketball, too. He
never misses a Cape Breton

Frankie's favourite foods

Frankie's favourite foods are pizza (pepperoni,
cheese, and meat lovers) and Chinese food (chicken
balls, rice, egg rolls, and almond soo gai). That's
why he always tells people to order their pizza and
their Chinese food before a big storm comes!

Highlanders game. These days, Frankie also goes to a lot of movies. His grandmother says he goes to all the movies at the local theatre.

Frankie got his first job in Grade 10, when his school required everyone to practice working at a real job for a couple of months (a lot of schools do this—it's called "work experience"). For his work experience, Frankie worked at Heather Bowling Lanes at Sydney Shopping Centre. It was an interesting job—Frankie got to help the manager fix the machine that sets up the bowling pins.

He got his next job a couple of years later, at the Mayflower Mall in Sydney. And he still works there today! Once a week, Frankie works as a custodian, cleaning windows and floors, and sanitizing the kids' rides. He's met a lot of people this way, and has a lot of friends at the mall. Even when he's

Fast Frankie Fact

Japan has more earthquakes than any other country in the world.

> **During blizzards, I stay indoors because it is too dangerous and there's usually zero visibility. That's why I warn people when there's a blizzard headed their way.**
> **— Frankie**

not working, he likes to go to the mall and talk to the other people who work there.

For a few years, Frankie had a second job. He spent so much time watching hockey at the rink that he was offered a job working there every Sunday. At first, Frankie turned it down—until he got home and found out that someone had told his dad about the whole thing.

When Frankie walked in the door at home, his dad asked him, "Did Kevin offer you a job?" and Frankie said, "Yes." His dad's response? "You'd better go back there and tell him that you want it." So Frankie did, and he worked at the rink every Sunday afternoon for about eleven years. Frankie's job was to clean up: he was responsible for cleaning the rink, including the bleachers, the penalty box, and the players' benches. He also had to take out the recyclables.

"That was another chance to be around other people," says Frankie's dad. "He would go to the rink every night and watch whatever was going on, skating or hockey, or whatever. I told him, well, you might as well go there and get paid for it."

Being a YouTube weather expert also gives Frankie the chance to connect with a lot of other people. Since so many of us enjoy his videos, he receives a lot of messages from fans around the world. He's inspired a lot of people, too.

When Frankie's first bobblehead came out in 2016, he did a signing at the Mayflower Mall. Lots of people came from Cape Breton, but some people also travelled from farther away to see him. Frankie remembers three people in particular: two kids who travelled from Halifax with their friend from Maine. The three children, who had travelled with a parent, were all autistic, and they wanted to meet Frankie because he's their hero. The kids introduced themselves, and Frankie chatted with them for a while. Guess what they wanted to know? What the weather was like in Halifax and Maine, of course!

Where do rainbows come from?
Sunlight is actually made up of a lot of different colours: red, orange, yellow, green, blue, indigo, and violet. You can't see them because when they're combined in the right way, they just look like white light. But when the light reflects off of raindrops in just the right way, the whole spectrum of colours separates, and for a little while you can see each one—as part of a beautiful rainbow.

ACKNOWLEDGEMENTS

IT TAKES A WHOLE BUNCH of people to make a book, and this one is no different. We would like to thank Frank MacDonald, Rose MacDonald, Hugh MacDonald, and Darlene MacDonald, who spent time sharing their memories, Pauline Simms for loaning us her journal, and Maynard Morrison for sending us his recording of Frankie's high school play. This book wouldn't be what it is without them.

We'd also like to thank Terrilee Bulger and Whitney Moran of Nimbus Publishing for supporting the project from the time it was just the tiniest seed of an idea. Thanks also to editor Whitney Moran for her pep talks and special ability to detect overly grown-up words, and for pulling us out of the weeds more than a few times. Thank you to Heather Bryan and her graphic design team for making the book a fun, colourful experience. Thanks to Lexi Harrington for doing so many of those necessary little things, from collecting author bios to orchestrating photo deliveries.

Thank you to Marc Muschler from Autism Nova Scotia for consulting with us on the sections related to autism. We value your help more than we can say.

Thank you to all of the fans who have helped make this such a happy story.

And finally, thank you to our families and friends, who support us always.

Frankie MacDonald and Sarah Sawler

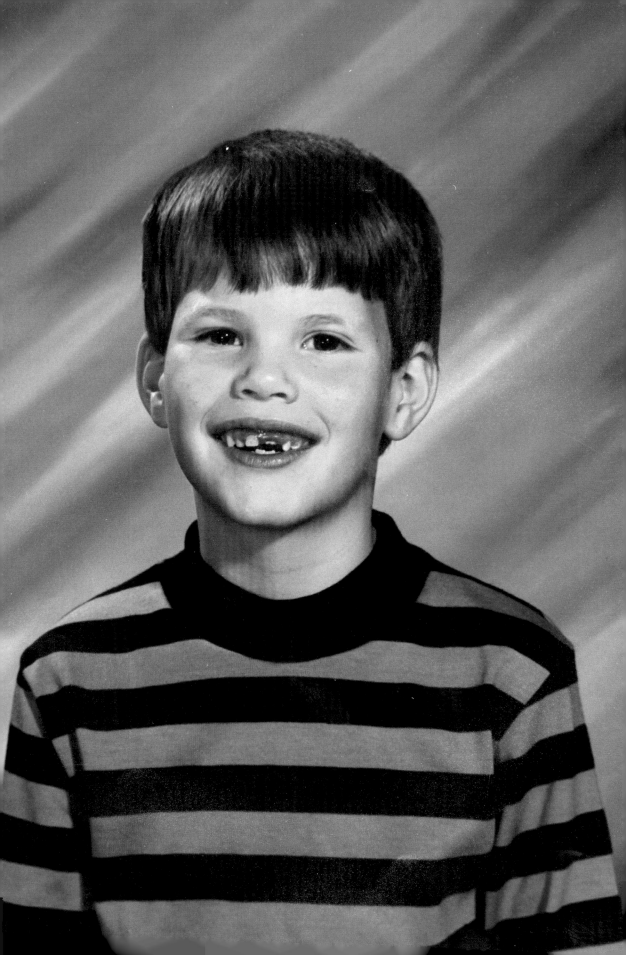

FRANKIE'S WEATHER QUIZ

By now you should know a thing or two about the weather. How many of these questions can you answer correctly? Check the bottom of the page to see how many you got right!

1–5 correct: Student of the Weather
6–8 correct: Weather Expert in Training
9–12 correct: Frankie MacDonald Seal of Approval!

1. A land-based, funnel-shaped storm is called:
a) hurricane
b) blizzard
c) tornado
d) tsunami

2. Which of these things don't help fight climate change?
a) drinking tap water instead of bottled water
b) turning off the tap when you brush your teeth
c) making sure your electronics are always plugged in
d) turning off the lights when you aren't using them

3. What should you NEVER do during a thunderstorm?
a) take a nap
b) swim in a lake
c) read a book
d) play a video game

4. A tsunami can be caused by an underwater:
a) volcanic eruption
b) landslide
c) earthquake
d) all of the above

5. Which of these is NOT a type of cloud?
a) cumulus
b) fluffostratus
c) altocumulus
d) nimbostratus

6. What year did we officially start naming Atlantic storms?
a) 1953
b) 1975
c) 2015
d) 1904

7. The largest ever _____ was discovered in Vivian, South Dakota, in 2010.
a) golf ball
b) mud puddle
c) hailstone
d) horse

8. Which location holds the world record for being the hottest place on earth?
a) Death Valley
b) Scorching Desert
c) Boiling Plains
d) Sizzling Island

9. Which country has more earthquakes than any other in the world?
a) Canada
b) Japan
c) Norway
d) Russia

10. The computer programs that help forecasters predict the weather are called:
a) super weather predictors
b) smart satellites
c) fantastic forecasters
d) weather models

11. When water droplets in the clouds get too heavy, this usually means:
a) a tornado
b) sunshine
c) rain
d) a blizzard

12. Geography is a branch of science that studies:
a) the science of earth's physical features, like mountains and lakes
b) the science of sound
c) the science of languages
d) the science of flags

Answers: 1c; 2c; 3b; 4d; 5b; 6a; 7c; 8a; 9b; 10d; 11c; 12a